D0708121

ROMEO AND JULIET

www.**transworld**books.co.uk

1   Why not 'Juliet and Romeo'? Critics note that this play is
    more about her, and her plight, than about him. And she
    has the best speeches: 'Romeo, Romeo! Wherefore art thou
    Romeo?' etc. The actor playing Juliet has the third-longest
    speaking part of all Shakespeare's women. One uses that
    word, 'woman' not 'girl' (although she must first have been
    played by a boy with an unbroken voice), because Juliet has
    wisdom, and fluency, far beyond her thirteen years.

The Incomplete Shakespeare

JOHN CRACE
ANNOTATED BY
JOHN SUTHERLAND

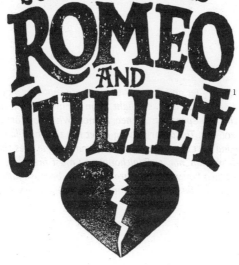

ROMEO AND JULIET[1]

Doubleday

LONDON · TORONTO · SYDNEY · AUCKLAND · JOHANNESBURG

DRAMATIS PERSONAE

CAPULETS

JULIET — thirteen-year-old girl; only child of the family. Yes, thirteen. Shakespeare wants us to remember it

CAPULET — her dad

LADY CAPULET — her mum (age: mid twenties; younger than dad, we can assume)

NURSE — formerly wet nurse, now personal attendant. Talkative

TYBALT — Juliet's cousin. Not talkative. Particularly after Romeo runs a sword through him

MONTAGUES

ROMEO — only son. Age indeterminate, probably sixteen. The heir

MONTAGUE — Romeo's dad; doddery

LADY MONTAGUE — Romeo's mum – not that you'd know it from the attention he pays her

BENVOLIO — Romeo's cousin (what's the Italian for 'wimp'?)

BALTHASAR — Romeo's 'man'. A useful dolt

THE PRINCE AND HIS ENTOURAGE

PRINCE ESCALUS Verona's Mr Big. Rarely picks up the right end of the stick

MERCUTIO Friend to all and anyone, except when swords are drawn

PARIS Young, feeble, unlucky

THE REST

FRIAR LAWRENCE Busybody

FRIAR JOHN A less busy body

SAMPSON, GREGORY, ABRAM Unimportant servants

MUSICIANS

APOTHECARY

CAPTAIN OF THE WATCH

2 *Star-crossed – really? We don't know nearly enough about Shakespeare the man, but on the evidence we have, we do know that he was not of the Mystic Meg faction. In* King Lear, *Gloucester, who is obsessed with astrological prophecy, is portrayed as an old fool. He misses what is going on in front of his eyes (before they are jabbed out). It's the unbridled gangsterism of Verona – the Crips and Bloods, Jets and Sharks – that destroys Romeo and Juliet.*

ACT 1

PROLOGUE

CHORUS
> Two households at war in fair Verona;
> The reckless Romeo takes for his wife
> Wan Juliet whose father doth disown her;
> A pair of star-cross'd lovers[2] take their life.
> Hear this sonnet as a warning précis
> Of a tale that shall become quite racy.

3   *There are some 175 puns in* Romeo and Juliet: *scores more than in any other play in the canon. Too many for some. I like them and the youthful exuberance they express.*

4   *The great critic Frank Kermode makes the point that these young lusties are speaking not just prose, but 'proletarian prose' – the language of the streets – even though they are 'well born'. Attune the ear.*

5   *Ho, ho! 'Maidenhead' = virginity, not a town in Berkshire (which Shakespeare would have passed through often enough on his trips from London to Oxford). Like 'codpiece' (see the knob jokes above), an inexhaustible source of juvenile humour. It can be wearing. But be indulgent: these are youngsters.*

ACT 1, SCENE 1

Verona, a public place

SAMPSON

See here the knob upon this door. Is't not the largest
knob thou ever saw?

GREGORY

Haven't you got anything better to do than tell
knob gags?[3]

SAMPSON

'Fraid not, old boy. 'Tis only our masters who may
talk in verse and so let's play this scene for banter.[4]

GREGORY

Then may we turn some maidens' heads or take
their maidenheads.[5]

SAMPSON

That's terrible.

GREGORY

It's better than anything a Montague would come up
with. Talking of which, here comes foul Abram.

Enter Abram

6   *Robert De Niro (in the famous* Taxi Driver *scene) is the apt allusion being made here by John Crace: 'You talkin' to me?' An Italian thing. De Niro was too old to play Romeo in the 1996 film version, so the casting directors chose his fellow Italo-American, Leonardo DiCaprio.*

7   *A modern critic would say there is a superfluity of bad testosterone in the Verona streets, and good testosterone between the Verona sheets. Shakespeare was not familiar with hormones and modern endocrinology, but he did believe in the four 'humours' (bodily secretions) and the 'temperaments' which they inspire: choleric, melancholic, sanguine, phlegmatic. It's 'choler' – hot-blooded anger – that is running freely in Verona. The English, unsurprisingly, are traditionally strong on 'phlegm'. Romeo, in the opening scenes, is 'melancholic'. Juliet, I would say, is 'sanguine' (hopeful and cheerful).*

ABRAM
Are you looking at me?[6]

SAMPSON
Are you looking at me?

ABRAM
Do you want to make something of it?[7]

They fight. Enter Benvolio

BENVOLIO
Put up your swords, you know not what you do.

Enter Tybalt

TYBALT
If there's a fight then I will to the fray.

BENVOLIO
Calm down, dear sir, it's powder puffs at dawn.

TYBALT:
Don't talk of peace, you're spoiling all the fun.
Without blood spilt, true meaning have I none.

They fight. Enter Capulet and Montague

CAPULET
Give me a crutch, I'll beat thee to a pulp.

8 Why are the Montagues and Capulets at daggers drawn?
   It's never made clear. An 'ancient grudge', we're told. One
   assumes it's something Italian, like a spat between Mafia
   families. Note how weak the Italian authorities are – gangs
   rule the streets of Verona. Not a cop in sight.

9 This is the first mention of Romeo in the play. Good mother
   that she is, with all this youth flashing steel, Lady Montague
   is worried about her boy. It reminds us that Romeo – although
   older than Juliet – is not fully grown.

10 Not really. Romeo is suffering (or pretending to suffer) from
   the 'malady of love'. A main element of 'courtship' as defined
   in Castiglione's manual, The Book of the Courtier (1528). The
   process of love was as intricate as the dance of the Sugar
   Plum Fairy.

MONTAGUE

I'd run thee through were not my knee so crook.

Enter Prince Escalus

PRINCE

Cease, I say, cantankerous old fools,
Thy deeds have made our streets a no-go zone.
No more shall Montagues and Capulets
Enact their *West Side Story*, Sharks and Jets,
Or else shall pay the forfeit of the peace.[8]

BENVOLIO

Methinks the prince doth have a valid point,
For as my name suggests, I'm naught but fair.

LADY MONTAGUE

O, where is Romeo? Saw you him today?[9]

BENVOLIO

Early this morn when I did walk abroad
I saw your son, but he did see me first
And he did leg it deep into the wood.

MONTAGUE

'Tis true he hath not been himself of late;
He stays awake at night and sleeps till noon,
Behaviour much like any teenager.[10]

11   It's sometimes shortened to 'coz'. More often than not, it just meant 'pal'. The equivalent today is 'bro'.

12   Modern audiences might think that Romeo, before his epochal meeting with Juliet, speaks with all the eloquence of a cuckoo in a cuckoo clock. In fact, as Elizabethan audiences would appreciate, Romeo is speaking straight, and long-windedly, from the Courtly Love rule book. It amused then more than it does now. But it's an important phase in the rapid growing-up of Romeo Montague.

13   The real reason he's being cagey, of course, is that she's a Capulet. A dynamite fact.

BENVOLIO

Leave it with me, I'll find out what's amiss.

Enter Romeo

BENVOLIO

Good morrow, cousin.[11]

ROMEO

Is that really the time?

BENVOLIO

What ails thee so that hours feel like days?

ROMEO

What further mooning must I do to prove
The sun it shineth not upon my love?
O hateful love, my love doth not requite
And makes me talk in rhyming opposites.[12]

BENVOLIO

What maid is this who breaks your heart in twain?

ROMEO

Alas I cannot bear to say her name,
To do so would my lust further inflame.[13]
Marry, Ben Vee, she doth refuse to wed;
No mini-mes to grace the marriage bed.

14 *Worth noting that most of Shakespeare's audience – the 'groundlings' – were probably not great readers or penmen. But when it came to listening, they were world-class. Better than us. The reason? The law required them to attend church and listen to long, complex sermons. Theirs was much more of a listening culture than ours. This is what freed Shakespeare to be not merely a dramatist, but a poet. Pinter and Beckett must have envied him.*

ACT 1, SCENE 2

Outside Capulet's mansion

PARIS
But now, my lord, what say you to my suit?

CAPULET
I would point out my girl is still thirteen,
Which e'en for Italy is still quite young.

PARIS
Come off it, sire, she's getting on a bit.

CAPULET
Then woo her, Paris, if thy love is strong,
But don't forget she is my only child,
And if she loves thee not then let her be.
Now I must attend to party planning;
My servant must make haste to tell the guests.

He hands invitations to his servant and leaves with Paris

SERVANT
How many times do I have to tell the old fool that
I can't read?[14]

Enter Benvolio and Romeo

15 *The most famous citizen of this city (if one goes back to the ninth century) is probably Pacificus of Verona. A great scientist, he is credited with the invention of the first public mechanical clock. It's relevant.* Romeo and Juliet *has the tightest, most precise time scheme of all Shakespeare's plays: four days, five nights. Everything in it can be timed: the play ticks and chimes with the passing minutes, hours and days. An interesting effect which audiences register but are not always aware of.*

BENVOLIO

I've full had my fill of lovesick gurning,
There's babes aplenty to indulge thy yearning.

ROMEO

Thou underestimates how truly deep
My depths are; deep so much I cannot sleep.

He takes a letter from the servant

'The Capulets invite you to their do,
There to meet my lady wife and daughter,
Not to forget my niece, fair Rosaline.'
Sounds great: tell me how to RSVP.

SERVANT

Just turn up at the Capulets' at about six.[15] As long as
you're not a Montague, there won't be any bother.

BENVOLIO

At last we'll get to see your Rosaline,
Whom thou lovest so much, thou dost not name.
I'll wager if thou join me at this bash
You'll meet some gorgeous babes who are more hot.

ROMEO

Once again thou dost assume me callow;
I'll come with thee: you'll not find me shallow.

16 A thirteen-year-old does not need a nurse. What we are
    meant to pick up is that the nurse was Juliet's wet nurse long
    ago in infancy. Juliet has no sisters, so the nurse is very close
    to her. A milk relative if not a blood relative. The nurse lost
    her maidenhead at twelve. Her daughter, Susan, died, and
    she became Juliet's wet nurse. This makes her twenty-five
    as the play begins. But as toothless as the babes she nursed.
    Wet nurses, because of the nature of their work, often had
    to malnourish their own offspring, thus, horrible thought,
    precipitating their death.

17 It's an Italian play – none of Shakespeare's more so. Why not,
    then, give Juliet the proper Italian name, 'Giulietta'? Because
    its five syllables (Jee-ool-ee-et-ta) would crowd out a ten-
    syllable line. All those Italianate vowels, with equal stress on
    every syllable. And Shakespeare, critics point out, probably
    liked the echo of 'jewel'.

18 Shakespeare was determined we should know that Juliet
    is only thirteen. The fact is repeated five times in the play.
    In modern times her juvenility, along with her love of sex
    (also stressed), is a huge production embarrassment. In the
    source for Romeo and Juliet (which Shakespeare faithfully
    followed), Arthur Brooke's abysmal three-thousand-line poem
    'The Tragicall Historye of Romeus and Juliet', she is sixteen.
    Why did Shakespeare clip three years off her age? Romeo is
    old enough to be banished, which means we may assume that
    he is over sixteen. The best date we can come up with for the
    first production of Romeo and Juliet is 1596–97, at which time
    Shakespeare (who had married a pregnant Anne Hathaway
    when he was eighteen) had a thirteen-year-old daughter.

ACT 1, SCENE 3

A room in Capulet's mansion

LADY CAPULET
  Nurse, where's my daughter? Call her forth to me.

NURSE
  I do remember that I was but twelve
  When I help'd you give birth to Juliet.[16]

Enter Juliet

JULIET
  Madam, I am here. Can you explain
  Why my name endeth not upon an A,
  Like other Giuliettas that I know?[17]

LADY CAPULET
  Think not to ask such unhelpful questions;
  Instead allow your thoughts to turn to love.

NURSE
  Often I think upon my long-dead Susan,
  Yet rejoice your Juliet still doth breathe.
  Do you remember how your husband laughed
  About her having sex when she was six?[18]

19 One of the more interesting puns that litter the early acts.
    'Marry!' (a 'low' allusion to the Virgin Mary) was a watered-
    down expletive – like 'Gee!' for Jesus. It was current in
    Elizabethan England, but less so than during the reign of
    her predecessor, Mary. 'Marry!' could be associated with
    Mariolatry – the Catholicism which, under Elizabeth's reign,
    could bring you to the stake with very warm feet. Friars, of
    course, were principally servants of the Catholic Church, and
    the friar has the third-longest part in the play. Shakespeare
    treads very carefully about such things. There is raging
    controversy about whether he was, covertly, a Papist (his
    father, John Shakespeare, probably was).

20 Lady Capulet herself bore Juliet when she too was thirteen,
    which means she was impregnated as early as twelve.

LADY CAPULET

Speak no more, that soundeth much too pervy,
Though marry,[19] 'marry' is the very theme
I came to talk of. Tell me, Juliet,
How do you feel about becoming wed?

JULIET

To tell the truth, I think myself too young.

LADY CAPULET

Well, think again; others younger than you
Are married every day within this town;[20]
The danger is you end up on the shelf.
Tonight look well on Paris: he has cash,
But wealth aside, he's also really hot;
Some say he doth possess the firmest bot.

JULIET

If it's your will, upon him I will look,
And if I like the likeness I shall act.

21 *Wordplay, we call it. But in the context of* Romeo and
    Juliet *it's more usefully thought of as verbal duelling – as
    aggressive as the swordplay it accompanies. Mercutio, who
    is a man of sense, is trying to jolly Romeo out of his absurd
    romantic posturing.*

ACT 1, SCENE 4

A street outside Capulet's mansion

ROMEO

    I do not feel like going out tonight,
    So being heavy, I shall bear the light.

MERCUTIO

    O dearest friend, you can be such a drag,
    If can't be fun at least be less profound;
    These opposites are getting on my nerves.

ROMEO

    If I be too moody for thine own mood
    Then go alone; I do not want to dance.

MERCUTIO

    If love be rough with you, be rough with love,
    Prick love for pricking and you beat love down.[21]

ROMEO

    You will not win me round by talk of pricks,
    My heart is set upon my killing joy.
    You hold your prick; I shall hold the candle.

22 Queen Mab (reach for your tissue) creeps up your nose at
    night and gives you dreams. Should be called Queen Sinusitis.
    Shakespeare seems to have invented her or picked her up
    from the superstitious old folks in Stratford. She inspires one
    of the great speeches in the play.

23 A timely word on Mercutio – one of the great parts in
    Shakespeare, much sought after by actors. He's neither
    a Capulet nor a Montague. He, as his name signals, is
    'mercurial' – Mercury is the flightiest (literally, he has wings
    on his heels) of the demi-divines. Mercutio moves between
    the feuding families like quicksilver (mercury), allying himself
    with neither, but bringing good sense wherever he drifts.

MERCUTIO

O now I see Queen Mab hath been with you;
She weaves her spider's web inside your dreams.[22]
Her worm doth eat away at happiness,
Thy serotonin levels record low.
I could and will go on at greater length,
Indulge me in this feat of imagery.

ROMEO

I beg you stop, my ears they start to bleed.

MERCUTIO

I can't, I won't, my verse is on a roll,
For dreams are naught but idle fantasies.[23]

ROMEO

OK, OK, I hear you, my good friend!
I'll come with you unto the bitter end
Of this night's revels. You go forth in mirth,
I with vile visions of my death foretold.

24 *Rosaline is one of the great unseens in Shakespeare. Interesting that she, like Juliet, is a Capulet, and, had Romeo persisted in his love of her, this play might well have been called* Romeo and Rosaline. *In picturing this scene, remember that the characters are masked, according to Italian festival practice. The women elaborately so. All Romeo can see is Juliet's eyes, and possibly her carefully coiffured hair. And those cherry-like lips.*

25 *The audience would have been aware – from poetry and plays – that there are two kinds of conventional love. Love of the eye, and love of the heart. Love of the eye is shallow –when Cupid's arrow strikes, it can happen in an instant (as it does here) between strangers across a crowded room. Love of the heart is slower-growing. Love of the head, making a third kind of love, is slower still.*

ACT 1, SCENE 5

Great hall in Capulet's mansion

CAPULET

    Welcome one and welcome all! Have a drink,
    And do not cease your dancing ere the dawn.

ROMEO

    What lady's that, which stands beside the wall?
    Her beauty glows and holds me in its thrall.
    My eyes forget the ugly Rosaline,[24]
    I shall not sleep until this girl is mine.[25]

TYBALT

    This, by his voice, sounds like a Montague;
    Fetch me my sword and I will run him through.

CAPULET

    Chill out, dear Tybalt, do not make a scene.
    'Tis Romeo, about whom all doth say
    He is a virtuous and well-govern'd youth.
    I do not want a ruck to spoil this night.
    You must endure him or yourself be gone.

TYBALT

    Patience I'll show and stay my tongue this once,
    But rest assured there'll be no second chance.

26 That tedious poeticising has dropped away. Romeo is now speaking 'nakedly', and does so throughout the rest of the play. A fine dramatic effect.

27 The couplet here denotes coupling. And copulation to come.

28 No, she doesn't. The nurse smells trouble – she's no longer a nurse (Juliet, young as she is, no longer needs nursing) but a minder. After that snogging, she certainly needs minding.

Exeunt Tybalt and Capulet

ROMEO
I am not worthy to embrace your hand,
My heart is thine, my arms in yours entwine.[26]

JULIET
Your chat-up lines are really none too grand,
But since you are so fit, they sound divine.

ROMEO
Then shall I kiss you firmly on the lips.

JULIET
And I shall hold thee by thy snake-like hips.[27]

They kiss

ROMEO
That was so nice, let us do it again.

JULIET
Come here, my prince, I thought you'd never ask.

They kiss again

NURSE
Madam, your mother craves a word with you.[28]

29 No one has convincingly explained why Rosaline was a
    member of the extended Capulet clan. Audiences have this
    in the back of their minds throughout – will Rosaline make
    a dramatic entry?

30 Not 'Who is that gentleman?' but 'What?'. That is, what
    family does he belong to? That is what will be all-important.

ROMEO

Who is her mother? I beg you fill me in.

NURSE

Her mother is the lady of the house.

ROMEO

That is bad news, for she's a Capulet.
I've gone and done it now. My death's assured.

BENVOLIO

Methinks thy short-term memory is shot
For was not Rosaline a Capulet?[29]
I did not hear you fearing for your life
When thou didst think you might make her your wife.

ROMEO

My friend, if nothing helpful can you say
'Tis best that nothing's said to spoil the play.

Exeunt Romeo and Benvolio

JULIET

Come hither, nurse. What is yond gentleman?[30]

NURSE

I know not.

31 *Everything is on a helter-skelter-fast timetable in this four-day play. Love of the eye has already become love of the heart.*

JULIET

    Go ask his name: if he be married,
    My grave is like to be my wedding bed.

NURSE

    His name is Romeo, and a Montague.
    'Twere best you asked his name before you kissed.

JULIET

    O whoops, that makes life trickier indeed;
    Trust me to lose my heart to th'enemy.[31]

NURSE

    It is a pretty pickle, that's for sure.

32 Dr Johnson, like most of us, regards this chorus as redundant. It's often dropped in performance – not least because the 'chorus' (in Greek drama it's a group of people; a 'chorus of one' is awkward) is half inside, half outside the play. Choruses rarely work well on the British stage. Programme notes with legs. Why did Shakespeare insert a second chorus? Perhaps because there were latecomers wandering in to the performance. Or perhaps it was intended as the dramatic equivalent of a break between rounds.

33 When he was in love with Rosaline, poetry and moping seemed quite enough for Romeo to be getting on with. But one of the gripping features of Romeo and Juliet, on page and stage, is the high-octane and unpredictable detonations of young lust when it's 'real'. It's disconcerting, because the lovers/lusters (let's just call them kids) are so extremely young. Shakespeare, a parent of similarly young children entering the storms of puberty, is, one may feel, exploring the concept of children taking early charge of their own destiny. And driving their parents and guardians crazy in the process.

ACT 2

PROLOGUE

CHORUS

It's time again to recap what you know:[32]
Poor Rosaline hath quickly been forgot,
Such are the ways of lovestruck Romeo
When close to Juliet, his senses shot.
Passion doth as passion will when lovers meet,
The brains go to the loins with kisses sweet.[33]

34 *The two big mansions in the action would be identified to the audience by hanging flags.*

35 *Since it's midsummer in Verona, baking by day and brilliantly starry by night, any cloud that crossed the heavens would indeed be lonely. Shakespeare wants us to be aware of the Italian heat. London tempers, too, were dangerously inflamed in the hot days of summer: air-con was centuries away.*

36 *The orchard – the most famous orchard in Shakespeare's drama – is richly symbolic. Fruitfulness (though the name of the month is never mentioned, it is July: the 'dog days') is in the air (literally, with the hanging, ripe apples; whether the juvenile Juliet is biologically 'ripe' is quite another question). Climbing over the wall hints at transgressions to come. Romeo is stealing Juliet in the same way a 'scrumping' lad steals apples. And, of course, there are the implications of 'forbidden fruit'. Eden, apples, primal sin and all that. And what (SPOILER ALERT) will come is a major surprise to the audience – not fornication but decent Christian marriage. Read on.*

37 *All the young men of Verona are – there is no other word – randy. But, as critic René Weis points out, Mercutio is 'the top predator in the sexual jungle'. Shakespeare wants us to register the fact that Romeo is, by contrast, 'courteous' – mannerly. We are invited to see Romeo throughout as a victim of love, not a sexual bandit. It's a vital distinction.*

ACT 2, SCENE 1

Outside Capulet's mansion [34]

ROMEO

Alone I wander, lonely as a cloud, [35]
My thoughts too great for this world or the next.

Exit Romeo
Enter Benvolio and Mercutio

BENVOLIO

Why jumps Romeo o'er the orchard wall? [36]

MERCUTIO

He is in love, though mainly with himself,
And with the thought of being so in love.
He pineth much for Rosaline's sweet eyes
Upon a whim, desire desireth quim.

BENVOLIO

Thou art quite harsh, yet also perhaps fair.

MERCUTIO

Trust me, Ben Vee, he's guided by his prick,
And pricks that pricketh rarely fail to bleed. [37]

38   There is an extended play here with a 'false aubade', which will go on throughout the whole scene. 'Aubade' = poetry inspired by dawn. It is, however, still darkest night at the moment. Shakespeare's theatre did not have lights or dimmers, hence it was impossible, with summery daytime performance, to create night-time gloom except by verbal reference. There are many such references in this scene. A nice mind-game is to fantasise about what Shakespeare would have done had he had a modern theatre, or a film studio, to work with. Oddly, his plays might ave been less poetic. No need for poetry when all you have to do is flip a switch.

39   Gown = nightgown. It is dark. But the gown (purest white, we assume) has an overtone of vestal (i.e. virginal) dress. It's both sexy and unsexy. We must keep that fact in mind, washed as our ears have been with Mercutio and the other lads' relentless bawdy talk.

40   We know tantalisingly little about the layout of an Elizabethan theatre. It is surmised that Juliet, in the performances during Shakespeare's day, appeared at the 'tiring window' – the small room above the acting area where actors would put on costumes. In the nineteenth century, with its more elaborate machinery and props, this window became a 'balcony', hence the famous balcony scene. The proxemics (i.e. where the actors are and their posture) are important. She is 'aloft'; he is looking up, as at the sun. Whose light would, of course, blind him were it real. Juliet (and Romeo) are only children, which is why she has a bedroom of her own where she can soliloquise without being overheard (except by the nurse, whom she has this evening sent away). Learned commentators on this scene have tied themselves in knots wondering how it is that Romeo sees Juliet before she actually 'appears aloft'. A heavenly vision?

41   The posture immortalised later by Rodin's statue of The Thinker. The technical term in Shakespeare's day is 'dumbshow' – the kind of physical language later used in silent movies. Elizabethan actors must have been skilled in it.

ACT 2, SCENE 2

Capulet's orchard

ROMEO
But soft! What light through yonder window breaks?
It is the east, and Juliet is the sun.[38]
She is more fair than any babe alive,
How I envy the gown in which she stands.[39]

Juliet appears aloft as at a window [40]

ROMEO
It is my lady, O, it is my love:
If only she did know how I do feel.
I know I can't stop going on and on
About the charms of my sweet Juliet,
But nothing else I have upon my mind.
I can but hope she feels the same as me.
See how she leans her cheek upon that hand!
Wouldst were that hand mine own.[41]

JULIET
                        Ay me!

ROMEO (*aside*)
                              She speaks!
Is there no end to Juliet's talents?

42 One of the more famous lines in the play, familiar even to those who have never seen or read it. 'Wherefore' is one of the words which, over the last four hundred years, we have learned to live without. It means more than just 'why'. The question it asks is, 'How did you become what you are?', or 'Where are you coming from?' It's interesting that, thirteen-year-old that she may be, Juliet is wholly ignoring family/paternal prohibitions. Parents are strangely feeble and powerless in this play. Adolescence rules. Good or bad?

43 Another very famous line. It's logically dubious given the associations which words carry with them. Call a rose 'shitwort' and the nostril would subliminally invoke something very un-sweet which might well complicate the sensory experience and probably alter what young men choose to give the objects of their love on Valentine's Day. What is interesting, however, is how much better a brain Juliet has than Romeo. This is a thirteen-year-old who has thought deeply about the philosophical implications of nominalism. Score one for the Italian primary-school system. The line is often quoted (there is reliable, but contradictory, textual justification) as 'by any other name'. Which I rather prefer.

44 He would, commentators agree, be very unlikely to bastardise himself. It's hyperbole, meaningless exaggeration. Forgivable in young lovers.

45 It's an interesting problem in production that, in order to be heard to each other, the couple must have raised their voices quite substantially. Not to put too fine a point on it, they are shouting. How have they done so without raising the alarm? It elevates the risk factor and audience excitement.

JULIET

O Romeo, Romeo! Wherefore art thou Romeo?[42]
By which I mean why art thou Montague
And not where art thou standing somewhere near?

ROMEO

She dost not know I'm here; I'll hold my tongue.

JULIET

'Tis but thy name that is my enemy;
What's in a name? That which we call a rose
By any other word would smell as sweet;[43]
If thou wert Smith how simple would it be
For me to shout aloud that I love thee.

ROMEO

Call me but love, and I'll be new baptised;
Henceforth I never will be Romeo.[44]

JULIET

What man art thou that thus bescreen'd in night
So stumblest on my counsel?

ROMEO

                                   Art thou deaf?
If I heard you, then surely you heard me?
I did clearly say the name Romeo.
But never mind, we'll let that defect pass.[45]
If thou findest my name a deal-breaker
Then gladly will I change it. Say the word!

46 *Love is strange. Remember that Juliet has never actually seen Romeo's face full on. On the earlier occasion they met, he was masked. Now it is shrouded, as he says, in night. There are plenty of willing maidens in Verona (as Mercutio and Benvolio never tire of reminding us). What magnetism draws Romeo and Juliet together?*

JULIET

Now I hear thee talking clear as day,
For thou hast stopped thy drippy mumblings.
Though I might wish thou weren't a Montague
You're perfect as you are, I'd change nothing.
Now tell me how you came here to these walls.

ROMEO

Love's wingèd chariot my legs did take
And sped me to the warmth of thine embrace.

JULIET

Thy poetry doth have a time and place,
But now there are some practicalities
On which to dwell. My kinsmen are quite fierce
And if they get a whiff of our intent
Thy heart from thy dear bod will soon be rent.

ROMEO

I have night's cloak to hide me from their sight.

JULIET

O there you go again and I do swoon,
For I do love thee more than sun or moon.
My legs do quiver when I hear thee speak,
Pray reassure me that you feel the same.
If thy love equals mine, I shall not cry.[46]

47 *A small shiver runs through the audience – the moon (whose shape changes every night) is proverbially emblematic of inconstancy. By invoking it, the slightest hint is introduced that Juliet may (as did Romeo with Rosaline) back out later on, as consequences become clearer.*

48 *One of the reasons the nurse is so present in the action is that the Capulets have put her there to keep an eye on their daughter. She has, however, a split loyalty. Bertolt Brecht wrote a sketch with her (desperate to see her lover) as the heroine, and Juliet as secondary. The nurse, comic and shrewd, has been given an interesting role by Shakespeare and good actresses of a certain age like playing the part.*

ROMEO

No tears are needed, sweetest Juliet,
For I do love thee with my heart and soul.

JULIET

I pray thou dost not mock me with thy words.
If falsehood be thy game, then leave right now.
Though darkness hides from thee my true desire
I fear I'm in too deep to back out now.
Swear by thy gracious self that thou lovest me.

ROMEO

I swear it loud and proud on bended knee.
Be not afraid of our whirlwind romance.

JULIET

Though still somewhat afeared. I do feel brave,
My bounty is as boundless as the sea,
I love thee to the stars and moon and back.[47]

Nurse calls from within[48]

JULIET

Make thyself scarce for now, I will be back.

Exit Juliet

ROMEO

Though blessed, I fear this might be all a dream;
But if it is, then I can live with that.

49 One of the points the play is at pains to get across is that although the couple's love is wild, it is not mad, or amour fou as the French call it (as it is, say, in A Midsummer Night's Dream). They will make plans to marry before going all the way. Critics make the point that there is a strong Christian morality running through the action.

50 Often quoted, soulfully – but what does it mean? Something along the lines of 'you only know the value of what you've got when you're about to lose it'. A beautiful platitude.

Enter Juliet

JULIET

   Though I must leave, I cannot stay away.
   If marriage be on offer, name the day.[49]

ROMEO

   Forsooth, my love, thou movest lightning quick,
   But I'm your man, I will return by nine.

NURSE

   Inside right now, you'll catch your death of cold.

JULIET

   Good night, good night! Parting is such sweet sorrow,[50]
   That I shall say good night till it be morrow.

51 *As noted earlier, the friar has the third-longest part in the play – it's often shortened since his garrulity clogs up the action and modern audiences lack the patience of their Elizabethan predecessors. It may be, of course, that Shakespeare wanted occasional strategic changes of pace. The friar is a Franciscan – a lover of nature – who has taken a vow of poverty (he's a mendicant, dependent on donations. There may be rather fewer in the future from the Capulet and Montague families). His knowledge of natural things, central to the plot, extends to the herbs, medicines and poisons to be found in the wild places around Verona. He is a bit of a witch doctor (and drug pusher); his knockout pills will be important in the action to come. Historically, the prominence given to the friar – and his undeniable good-heartedness – encourages the line of criticism that Shakespeare was sympathetic to Catholicism. This, in a country as rigorously Protestant as Elizabethan England, could only be expressed with great care. Stage performers typically weigh up carefully how they will 'play' Friar Lawrence.*

52 *Friar Lawrence is Romeo's confessor. One of the teasing elements in the play is Shakespeare's apparent sympathy for Catholicism. As mentioned above, it was something to be careful about in Elizabeth's reign (the play, recall, was performed, as we can best calculate, six or seven years before her death) – particularly, as every thinking person realised, at the end of that glorious era. There were Catholic contenders for the throne aplenty.*

ACT 2, SCENE 3

Outside Friar Lawrence's cell

FRIAR LAWRENCE

Pim pom, pim pom, pim pom piddle aye ay,
Though jolly might I sound, words of truth I say.
While gathering divers plants eclectic
I mull over matters dialectic:[51]
Virtue itself turns vice, being misapplied;
And vice sometimes by action dignified.

Enter Romeo

ROMEO

Good morrow, father.

FRIAR LAWRENCE

                 Benedicite!
It seems to me that thou art knackerèd,
I do suspect you have not been to bed.
Most likely supping at the holy shrine
Of love's young dream, thy sweetest Rosaline![52]

ROMEO

Why that's not fair, that girl is dead to me,
Far from her arms I have found remedy.

53 It is not Juliet who has entranced him, of course, but the
   wayward lad Cupid, whose arrows fly randomly. Friar
   Lawrence, like Romeo's buddies Benvolio and Mercutio, is
   forever trying to talk sense to Romeo – whom, it would seem,
   everyone in Verona loves. There are people like that.

54 The reason the friar flouts Church disciplines – not to
   mention the rights of the two families to 'give away' their
   children – is that he believes marrying the couple secretly will
   be a kind of conflict resolution and will create peace between
   the Montagues and Capulets. One hopes he's a better botanist
   than peacemaker.

FRIAR LAWRENCE

    I confess, this I do find surprising;
    What of thy confession am I missing?

ROMEO

    Then plainly know my heart's dear love is set
    On the fair daughter of rich Capulet.
    So I've come to you on this precious day
    To beg you have us married right away.

FRIAR LAWRENCE

    Hold on, hold on! Let us go back a bit.
    Last week you said that Rosaline was it;
    Now she is dumped without another thought,
    And in a new amour you're happ'ly caught.

ROMEO

    I beg you, father, give me not such hell,
    For I am caught within a lover's spell.[53]

FRIAR LAWRENCE

    Relax, my son, for I will see thee right.
    Your wedding may two houses yet unite.[54]

55 *There was considerable formal ceremony associated with a duel. Tybalt is distantly related to the Capulets – and the house's honour he takes to be his honour. He has been a loomingly threatening figure ever since he and Romeo fell out during the ball. He must have a good radar, though. Only the lovers and Friar Lawrence know that marriage (and with it a huge insult to the Capulet clan) is afoot.*

56 *Bawdy joke (as if we didn't have enough of them from these two incorrigibly filthy-mouthed chatterers). 'Cazzo' is 'prick' (penis) in street Italian. 'Ragazzo' = youth.*

ACT 2, SCENE 4

A street in Verona

MERCUTIO
Where the devil should this Romeo be?

BENVOLIO
Not at his father's house, so don't ask me.

MERCUTIO
Shall we quit all this talking-in-verse stuff for a
few moments?

BENVOLIO
Good plan. Have you heard Tybalt's sent a letter
to lover boy challenging him to a duel?[55]

MERCUTIO
Romeo is already as good as dead to us, impaled
on the shaft of his own love pump.

BENVOLIO
Snarf! Snarf!

MERCUTIO
In any case, Tybalt has the campest swordsmanship.
On guard, get you! This *ragazzo* is a *cazzo*.[56]

57 *Ominous and prophetic. Dido was a tragic lover. The Queen of Carthage, she became Aeneas's lover. She committed suicide when he left her. Allusions such as this stick in the mind. The way in which she killed herself is significant (see note 153).*

58 *It reminds us how little actual physical contact there has been between the lovers – none privately. 'Goose', incidentally, was low slang for 'woman'. In London slang, 'geese' meant 'prostitutes'. The audience would have picked that up.*

BENVOLIO

That's enough of the non-PC gags.

Enter Romeo

ROMEO

Good morrow to you both.

MERCUTIO

Ooh look at you all doey-eyed and mooning.
Compared to thy gorgeous babe, Dido must have
been a right dog.[57]

ROMEO

Give it a rest, pal. I'm not in the mood for all
this right now.

MERCUTIO

Diddums. When I do talk of love you come out
in goose bumps. Tell me, have you been goosing
your lover's bumps?[58]

ROMEO

You don't half go on.

Enter nurse

NURSE

Can anyone tell me where I can find a man
called Romeo?

59 Romeo identifies himself because he does not know the nurse, and can't immediately perceive the danger of revealing who he is to someone who can take the information straight to the Capulets – at the risk of his life and his hopes for a relationship with Juliet.

60 Loose Capulet's top gun, Tybalt, on him, she implies.

61 The first reference to where the marriage will take place. No caterers or wedding planner required.

62 The nurse is now a co-conspirator. She cannot, from this point on, expect a long career in the Capulet mansion.

ROMEO

You've just found him.[59]

NURSE

A word in your ear, please.

Exeunt Benvolio and Mercutio

NURSE

I'll say this once and once only. My mistress is a good
girl and if you mess with her I'll mess with you.[60]

ROMEO

Ungentle nurse, I could not love her more,
We shall be wed in Friar Lawrence's cell
Before the day is out, that is for sure.[61]
A ladder will I send to thee at home
So I may climb to get my Juliet.

NURSE

Fair enough. See you later.[62]

63 See note 15 about the unusual clock-driven nature of the play's plot. It's like Edgar Allan Poe's 'The Pit and the Pendulum' – every minute the swishing axe comes closer to the lovers' throats, did they but know it.

64 The nurse talks too much – and much of what she says is nonsense (something Shakespeare wants us to register). It's July in Italy. Cold?

65 To quote Mel Brooks's joke: 'men in tights'. Close-fitting hose showed off a young man's calves. Like the codpiece, it was thought to be alluring.

ACT 2, SCENE 5

Capulet's mansion

JULIET

O where is nursey, why is she not back?
She is already seven minutes late.[63]
For love's young dream, time passeth really quick,
And yet she dawdles on her aching pins.

Enter nurse

JULIET

Ah there you are, you've kept me waiting long.
Didst thou find Romeo? What did he say?

NURSE

Hang on a mo, I need to catch my breath,
It's cold outside, I nearly caught my death.[64]

JULIET

Don't mess with me, pray tell me all your news.
I need to know that my love playeth true.

NURSE

As it happens I did meet your Romeo.
And very well he seems and nice legs too.[65]

66 Note that the nurse uses the informal 'thee', not 'you' –
confirming that, now that she is in on the great marriage
plan, she is an equal. Elizabethan ears would pick up the
meaningful vocative.

JULIET

    Enough, enough. No more of this wordplay,
    Just spit it out, for I can wait no more.

NURSE

    'Tis my bunions that playeth up the most;
    Much more of standing, I'll give up the ghost.

JULIET

    Thou driv'st me mad with all this foolery.
    Thine aches and strains are nothing to my pain.

NURSE

    Very well, my Juliet, I'll tell thee straight:
    Hie you to church, and there you shall be wed;
    Romey doth feel exact the same as thee.[66]
    I must depart, a ladder must I fetch;
    Thy work be done tonight. Nudge nudge, wink wink.

67 Lawrence's speech is littered with Veronese thoughts for the
    day. He's a walking Elizabethan motto calendar. Shakespeare
    intends us to pick up on the stale hand-me-down quality of his
    moralising.

68 Betrothal was contractual, not verbal; the lovers have skipped
    that preliminary ceremony. The friar is not (by Elizabethan
    standards) breaking the law. Boys could be married at
    fourteen, girls at twelve. But, that young, it was almost always
    a business transaction, or like moving pawns on a chessboard.
    The marriage could be annulled if not consummated. The
    Elizabethans believed that the best time to marry was before
    noon (making time for what would happen that night). That,
    we may assume, is why the clock is ticking here.

69 NB: Shakespeare does not show the ceremony on stage. The
    royal-appointed censor, the Lord Chamberlain, would have
    been down on him like a ton of bricks for blasphemy had
    he done so. Particularly as it would have been a Catholic
    ceremony, largely in Latin.

ACT 2, SCENE 6

Friar Lawrence's cell

ROMEO

I cannot wait to have her in my sight:
Then love-devouring death do what he dare;
It is enough I may but call her mine.

FRIAR LAWRENCE

Passions that brightly burn are quickly spent;
'Tis often best to take things nice and slow.[67]
Not that thou hears a word, thine ears are closed,
For here comes Juliet, thy true betrothed.[68]

Enter Juliet

ROMEO

Ah Juliet, my love is like a rose:
It opens up to thee and I do swear
That I adore you more each passing hour.

JULIET

Such fancy talk from you is very well,
Yet I to language tend more down to earth,
I can't sum up my sum in poetry.

FRIAR LAWRENCE

Come, come with me, the pair of you be wed,
Wait an hour more, you both will be a-bed.[69]

70   *Another reminder that these are the 'dog days' of July, when the temperature drives the dogs in the streets to murderous frenzy. Benvolio, we are to assume, is something of a coward by nature. Or perhaps just sensible beyond his years among all the yapping, snarling and fighting.*

71   *I.e. a gang of their hell-raisers.*

72   *He does not want every Tomaso, Riccardo and Enrico being able to talk about the Romeo and Juliet business. It's private.*

ACT 3, SCENE 1

Verona, a public place

BENVOLIO

I pray thee, good Mercutio, let's retire:
On this dog day, we're sure to fight as dogs.[70]

MERCUTIO

You're such an old fusser. I'm sure we can get
through a day without a brawl.

BENVOLIO

But what if we meet the Capulets?

MERCUTIO

Then we meet the Capulets. We don't have to fight
them unless you pick a fight with them.

Enter Tybalt

BENVOLIO

Here are the Capulets.[71] Who would have guessed?

TYBALT

Oi, stop a while; a word into thine ear.[72]

MERCUTIO

What do you want?

73 A calculated insult: 'villain' means not just 'wrong-doer', but 'low-born'. The word rankles. Romeo is noble.

74 If he can provoke Romeo into drawing first, he can plead self-defence and not stand trial for assassination. Contract killing. Romeo is unwilling to fight because, after what happened just a few hours ago, Tybalt is now his kinsman. Directors sometimes suggest that Tybalt (a character of few words) merely wanted honourable swordplay, not bloodshed. Perhaps a small flesh wound.

TYBALT

You're mates with Romeo, aren't you? Tell me
where he is.

MERCUTIO

Go and find him yourself.

Enter Romeo

TYBALT

No need, for by coincidence he's here.
Romeo, the hate I bear thee can afford
No better term than this – thou art a villain.[731]

ROMEO

I am a man in love and therefore can't
Say more than hello trees and daffodils.
I do protest I never injured thee.
Calmer, karma; I cannot villain be.

TYBALT

Take out your sword, I'm desperate to fight.[74]

ROMEO

If it's OK by you, I'll keep mine sheathed.

MERCUTIO

Well fuck me sideways; if Romeo isn't up for a
ruck then I certainly am.

75   He dies with a universal curse. His key word is relevant.
     Summer outbreaks of plague regularly closed the London
     theatres for long or short periods. A number of the audience
     would be holding pomanders (oranges stuffed with cloves)
     to their mouths to avoid infection from neighbours' breath.
     (There was no need. The plague was communicated by fleas.
     They should have held their pomanders to their armpits.)

76   Hope against hope. Romeo desperately does not want a death,
     and gang war, to get in the way of his imminent marriage.

77   He hopes for the benefit of clergy, but death comes first.
     Where is that Friar Lawrence when you need him?

Tybalt and Mercutio fight

ROMEO
Hold, Tybalt! Good Mercutio.

Mercutio is mortally wounded

MERCUTIO
I am hurt.
A plague o' both your houses.[75] I am sped.

ROMEO
Chin up, old boy, it looks like just a scratch.[76]

MERCUTIO
'Tis a bit more than that, I think you'll find;
Find me a bed where I can lie me down.[77]

Exeunt Mercutio and Benvolio

ROMEO
I fear my courage has dissolved and that
My love for Juliet has made me wet.

Enter Benvolio

BENVOLIO
O Romeo, Romeo, brave Mercutio's dead!

78 I.e. 'quick' in the sense of 'alive' (as in 'the quick and the
    dead'). It's never too late, or too serious, for a pun.

79 The cops ('watchmen') are being called – few and far between
    as they are in Verona (it is citizens who intervene to stop the
    fray). The prince, as judge and jury, will come down heavily
    on street murder. Benvolio, as throughout, embodies sensible
    timidity. No one listens. His name means 'well-meaning'.

ROMEO

That was quick. My friend's no longer quick.[78]
Now that I'm angry, I will Tybalt fight.

They fight. Tybalt dies

BENVOLIO

Now you've gone and done it. Blood has spill'd
And you must scarper hence or yours will too.[79]

Exit Romeo
Enter Prince, Lady Capulet and Montague

PRINCE

Where are the vile beginners of this fray?

BENVOLIO

O noble prince, jump not to conclusions.
Though lyeth Tybalt dead 'twas his own fault.
He picked a fight and slew Mercutio;
Romeo took revenge and that's God's truth.

LADY CAPULET

He bears false witness. He is Montague.
I beg Romeo be condemned to death.

MONTAGUE

'Tis clear Ben Vee's account is accurate,
Be fair to Romeo and let him live.

80 *Like the friar (marrying the lovers in his cell, after a three-day courtship which would make Speedy Gonzalez look like a slowcoach), the prince does not stand on ceremony in this street trial. His aim, with the excessively lenient sentence on Romeo (who was acting in revenge, not self-defence), is political, hoping to cool off a threatening war between the two most powerful houses, and their gangster youngsters, in Verona's streets. Again we hear the ticking clock. If he wants to live, Romeo must leave town by sundown (in July it falls at around nine thirty). He has other business in mind that night, of course. The marriage is as yet unconsummated. The audience is in suspense.*

PRINCE

I've pondered all and now my judgment make:
Romeo slew him, he slew Mercutio;
Two wrongs don't make a right. For that offence
Immediately we do exile him hence.[80]

81 We are reminded she is still a virgin. Were Romeo to leave
    town, the marriage could be as quickly annulled as it was
    made on grounds of non-consummation. This fact will be
    in the forefront of the audience's mind. Things hang in the
    balance. Romeo left Juliet, after the ceremony, to inform his
    pals, we assume – and, who knows, possibly his family (whom
    he is never seen talking to) – of what dire thing he has done
    with the forlorn hope that it will establish peace between the
    houses. No such luck.

82 The nurse has been long enough in the Capulet household to
    be fonder of Tybalt than Romeo. Her job is at risk – something
    that will have crossed her ever-materialistic mind.

ACT 3, SCENE 2

Juliet's room in Capulet's mansion

JULIET

This day I've had enough of: bring me night
And with it Romeo here to my side.
In the darkness I would ward his wood
With modesty he take my maidenhood.[81]
Give me my Romeo, and when he shall die,
His face, like stars, shall light up the night sky.

Enter nurse

NURSE

We are undone, lady, we are undone!
Alack the day! He's gone, he's kill'd, he's dead![82]

JULIET

What devil art thou, that dost torment me thus?
If my true love is dead, I cannot cope.
Hath Romeo slain himself? Is that the truth?
For if it is, 'twere best I followed suit.

NURSE

O Tybalt, Tybalt, such a charming bloke,
I scarce can bear to tell thee he has croaked.

JULIET

What news is this? Buy one death, get one free?

83 Not yet – until the defining nocturnal act – her husband.

84 'Bastard'? Juliet imagines that the Montagues will disown
    him. Life could be difficult thereafter. No one of their noble
    class works for a living.

85 William of Occam (1287–1347) was a Franciscan monk, like
    Lawrence. He was also a philosopher, unlike Lawrence, who
    – we may well think – has barely two ideas to rub together
    under his tonsure. Basically, what the 'razor' recommended
    was that if there are two competing theories or choices,
    always go with the simpler. The mention of 'razor' raises the
    question: are the young blades in Verona bearded or not?
    Beards were fashionable in Elizabethan times and were cut
    in various styles, including pointed, square, round or oblong.
    Starch was applied to keep them in place.

86 A woman, on marriage, became her husband's chattel, or
    spousal property. Juliet (Juliet Montague as she now is) has
    transferred allegiance. There is also a hint here that Juliet
    knew that Tybalt had gone into the streets looking for Romeo.

87 Suicide now hangs, like a black cloud, over the action of the
    play, and in this scene is specifically forecast. One should
    remember the awful consequences (outlined in Hamlet).
    The 'self-murdered' were, by law, excommunicated, and
    routinely buried at crossroads, where they were thrown into
    a pit without religious ceremony and sometimes staked,
    like vampires, to the dirt (a cruel addition, to forestall
    resurrection on the Day of Judgment). Things are very serious.

88 This will be Juliet's cover story when the whatever hits the
    whatever. A climax, so to speak, is building.

NURSE

Tybalt is dead, with Romeo to blame,
And he that kill'd him is now banishèd.

JULIET

Why that's not quite so bad as I had feared;
For though I'm cross my kinsman has been killed
And that his blood lies on Romeo's hands
At least my fiancé is still alive.[83]

NURSE

I always said he wasn't worth your while,
I'm not the least surprised he's turn'd out vile.

JULIET

How very dare you talk of him like this?
A bastard he may be,[84] yet he is mine
And mine alone to curse and hate; not thine.
Yet I can hate him not for he was truly caught
Upon a razor Occam ne'er conceived.[85]
My husband lives that Tybalt would have slain,
And Tybalt's dead that would have slain my husband.[86]
Thus it is a lose-lose situation.
There is no happy ending I can see;
I'll take a rope and from this window hang,
And death, not Romeo, take my maidenhead![87]

NURSE

Stop thy self-pity now and get a grip;
I'll find Romeo hidden in a cell
And send him to your chamber for farewells.[88]

89 Romeo, having killed Tybalt, ran off. He has been by himself
    – but where? Doing what? One assumes he has been in the
    woods outside the city, talking to no one, in a condition of
    confusion and indecision. Wondering how he can run away to
    the neighbouring city-state of Mantua and still have his Juliet.
    Friar Lawrence, who was not a witness to the recent street
    bloodbath, has nonetheless heard the prince's proclamation,
    announced by a caller through the city, that 'Romeo is
    banished, and should be killed on sight if found in Verona
    after nightfall' – which is getting closer by the minute.

90 A lame pun. But the image is of flies buzzing around a dead
    body. Romeo assumes (it will be an important plot element
    later) that, without him, Juliet will kill herself.

ACT 3, SCENE 3

Friar Lawrence's cell

ROMEO

Father, what news? What is the prince's doom?

FRIAR LAWRENCE

Not the best, I grant thee, yet panic not.
The upside is thy life is thine to keep;
The bad news is that thou art banished
And must Verona leave before nightfall.[89]

ROMEO

Banishment is more cruel than purgatory;
I'd rather die than live without my love.

FRIAR LAWRENCE

If thou wert sane, thou wouldst regret those words;
The prince hath shown thee mercy, don't be dim.

ROMEO

'Tis torture, and not mercy. Can't you see
That this is all about me, me and me?
Dost thou not understand my banishment
Is like unto the stars from heaven rent?
Flies may buzz around my Juliet's face
Yet from such beauty I am forced to fly.[90]

91 *Another of those usages one is sorry to have lost. It is the conversationally shortened form of 'I pray thee' – more courteous than 'please', indicating a degree of deference.*

FRIAR LAWRENCE

A drama from a crisis thou dost make,
But while thou dost still pun there must be hope.

ROMEO

It is no good, you cannot cheer me up,
I throw me to the ground with heavy sobs.

Enter nurse

FRIAR LAWRENCE

Prithee[91] stand up, the nurse would speak with you.

ROMEO

I won't, I won't, she can talk to my back.

NURSE

What is Romeo doing on the floor?

FRIAR LAWRENCE

He thinks it doth make him tormented look.

NURSE

My mistress is the same, she weeps and weeps;
Now quit your blubbing, sir, we need to talk.

Romeo rises

92 He uses the informal 'thou' ('you' is more common in his speech to the friar), stressing the fact that the nurse is, however involved in confidential matters, still a servant. 'Spoke you' would be what he would say to an equal. Democracy has robbed the English language of these fine social distinctions. Sadly, some think. What dost thou?

By this point in the play, most members of the audience will have come round to feeling that, on the whole, the Montagues are a nicer sort of family than the Capulets. Both families, we note, are clients of the friar – though he, too, seems to be more on Team Montague.

93 Does he mean it? The point has been made (not least by her incessant complaints) that the nurse is a rickety old biddy. What is happening here, interestingly, is that Romeo is regressing into childishness. Note, in passing, that swords are used by Romeo's class (there were prohibitions on commoners being armed) for killing other people; daggers ('the bare bodkin', as Hamlet calls it) were useful for killing oneself – the 'Roman death'. The young nobles in Verona would be carrying rapiers – fashionable weaponry – and would have been trained in the intricate, almost balletic use of them in duels. Their 'men' (lower-class henchmen) would be carrying simpler, more obviously lethal weaponry (sometimes just a club, or cosh). It's not clear that Tybalt wanted anything more than a show encounter with Romeo, and perhaps a harmless nick or two, before everything went wrong.

94 Sensible advice. Let it all die down, then come back. But this is a play where everything moves at high speed.

ROMEO

Spake thou of Juliet?[92] How is it with her?
Doth she not think of me a murderer?
I hath spoiled our joy ere we had a chance
To love as lovers will in ignorance.

NURSE

Nothing hath she said, nor nothing will
Until she doth stop sobbing all the time.

ROMEO

I blame myself, I know it is my fault.
I see a knife conveniently placed
And with its trusty blade I will self-harm.[93]

Nurse seizes the dagger

FRIAR LAWRENCE

Stop all these girly tears, I've had enough
Of morbid self-indulgent theatrics;
Remember that thy Juliet still lives
As do you, though heaven knows I'm tempted
To do you in myself, once and for all.
Now fly to her and give a farewell kiss.
Thence go to Mantua and face exile.
In time the prince with thee will reconcile.[94]

95 *The union with Paris is a political, arranged thing. By
marrying off Juliet to Paris, the Capulets are aiming to form
an alliance with the prince – whose kinsman Paris is. Hints
suggest he is not a whole lot older than her. Typically, very
young children were involuntarily married off in the interests
of their elders.*

ACT 3, SCENE 4

Capulet's mansion

CAPULET

Things have turned sour, sir, and no mistake;
My daughter is upset by Tybalt's death,
So cannot see you on this wretched night.[95]

PARIS

These times of woe afford no time to woo,
I won't presume to marry her tonight.

CAPULET

That's very kind, I do appreciate
How much thy noble ardour is restrained.
If you could give it two days, maybe three,
Then Juliet will be as right as rain.

96 *As everyone in the audience will appreciate, she wants him to make love to her again. The second coming, as irreverent young men (like the sadly departed Mercutio) would say. Something we are to assume has happened at least once in the intervening hours. It is morning. Was it Romeo's plan, all along, to spend the night with Juliet and consummate their marriage (thereby preventing her union with Paris)? Or did he get carried away?*

97 *They croon to each other, like the proverbial turtle doves. The duet delicately implies they are now, at last, truly united – flesh of each other's flesh. The big question 'Now what?' has been temporarily postponed.*

98 *A submerged pun, and an important one – 'die' brings to mind a synonym for sexual climax. 'The little death', it was called. Romeo is here slyly promising more of the same. But what, we must wonder, is his plan? We are now in the area of what is called, in literary criticism, Liebestod – a useful German word for love + death. The only way Romeo and Juliet can preserve this sublime moment in its full perfection is by not growing old and grey, but dying while they are still young. Shakespeare builds up to this tragic inevitability. There are no happy ever afters on offer, we are beginning to realise.*

ACT 3, SCENE 5

Juliet's bedroom

JULIET

I beg you, leave me not, 'tis far too soon; 'Tis not the
birds that sing, it is the nurse;
Dawn breaketh not, the light it is the moon.[96]

ROMEO

Thou speak'st so sweet, I quite forget thy age;
Never a girl of thirteen have I met
Who art so old in body and in thought.[97]

JULIET

Suspend belief and let me be thy wife,
Don't leave my side; I yearn to hold thee tight
To my sweet bosom and ne'er let thee go.

ROMEO

Then will I stay, e'en though the dawn has come,
And smother thee in kisses passionate.
And if I captured be, then let me die.[98]

Enter nurse

NURSE

Your lady mother is coming to your chamber.

99 An appropriate farewell, meaning 'as God wills'. The next time they meet will be in the afterlife.

100 Lady Capulet's error reminds us that Romeo is a convicted killer as well as her son-in-law (did she but know it).

Exit nurse

ROMEO
On second thoughts, my love, it might be best
Were I to leave right now and say adieu.[99]

JULIET
Then go, sweet Romeo, yet still I fear
That thou wilt end up dead within a tomb.

Romeo climbs down the ladder. Enter Lady Capulet

LADY CAPULET
Why, how now, Juliet!

JULIET
                                        Madam, I am not well.

LADY CAPULET
'Tis good to weep and grieve thy cousin's death,
Yet enough, enough be. Therefore have done.

JULIET
I cannot choose but ever weep the friend.

LADY CAPULET
You fail to understand your state of mind:
Thou weep'st that he who Tybalt killed still lives.[100]

101 *Interesting that Lady Capulet knows where Romeo will hide out till the heat dies down. Has the nurse told her? For obvious reasons, it's not a fact that Romeo would want universally known. Mantua is the nearest town to Verona – some thirty miles distant. Given the disunited nature of Italy at the time, it had its own structures of authority. It was, if anything, a grander town than Verona and in a state of constant rivalry with it.*

102 *Juliet is in an interesting quandary here. For family consumption, she has declared a hatred for Romeo – killer of her cousin Tybalt (whom she, too, was fond of). But she cannot marry Paris. So she slips out the reason why she can't marry him deceitfully: 'I hate that awful Romeo, but I'd rather marry even Romeo than Paris.' Self-assertion is useless, however. She can be forced to marry whoever her father decides she should marry. If he wishes, he can beat her all the way to the altar.*

JULIET *(aside)*
> She speaks the truth better than she doth know.
> God pardon him! I do, with all my heart;
> Would none but I might venge my cousin's death.

LADY CAPULET
> Fear not, my daughter, vengeance will be ours.
> I'll track the villain down in Mantua
> And have Romeo poisoned in a bar.[101]

JULIET
> I wish Romeo nothing less than sleep,
> His eyes to close for ever next to mine.

LADY CAPULET
> Cheer up, old thing, I do bring thee good news:
> In three days to Paris thou shalt be wed.

JULIET
> Over my dead body, it will not be;
> I will not marry yet, and, when I do, I swear,
> It shall be Romeo, whom you know I hate,
> Rather than Paris. Suck on that, Madam.[102]

LADY CAPULET
> Here comes your dad, now say that to his face.

Enter Capulet and nurse

103 *One wonders, as the action unwinds, about the sexual*
     politics of the play. The older generation (older? Recall
     that Lady Capulet is only in her mid twenties) are tyrants.
     Patriarchy rules in Verona. Yet Romeo and Juliet, in their
     dealings with each other and in their very short marriage,
     treat each other as equals. Indeed, Juliet is sometimes the
     dominant member in their brief union. SPOILER ALERT: One
     of the ironies to come, in the tragic conclusion, is that the
     older, parental generation have learned nothing.

CAPULET

    There, there, my Juliet, let not thy tears
    Stain thy pale cheeks. For as a tempest reigns,
    So it seems calmer when your pa's around.
    Now has your mother told you the good news?
    Your wedding has been fixed for this Thursday.

JULIET

    For this kind offer, I do give thee thanks,
    But regret that I am otherwise engaged.

CAPULET

    'Tis not the kind of thanks I want to hear.
    No more of Mister Nice Guy will you hear,
    I'll drag thee to the church, ungrateful bitch.

NURSE

    She's not so bad, do not abuse her so.

CAPULET

    And you can shut up too. If help I need,
    I'll ask for it. Till then pray hold thy tongue.[103]
    My mood is foul; all of you beware,
    I am not used to being disobeyed.
    This I swear: I shall disown my daughter
    Unless she will act as a daughter oughta.

Exeunt Lord and Lady Capulet

104 Wise advice. But from this point on, the nurse is Juliet's enemy. Things are falling apart in Verona very fast.

105 If the friar has no remedy, she will kill herself and go to hell for it. She believes that. The audience shivers sympathetically. Eternity is a long time to suffer for one night's bliss.

JULIET

O help me, nurse – what a mess I'm in:
My husband is on earth, my faith in heaven;
How can this be resolved except in death?
What sayest? Hast thou no words of comfort?

NURSE

'Tis tricky, Madam, that I'll not deny.
Romeo is banished; even were he safe
There's little chance of him returning here
By stealth and shacking up with you.
Forget Romeo; he is dead to thee,
Opt for a quiet life and Paris wed.[104]

Exit nurse

JULIET

Well, thanks a lot for nothing, you old bag,
That's the last time I trust thee with my life.
Instead I'll hie me to the friar's cell;
If he can't make things well, then bring on hell.[105]

106 *The friar is squirming here. He has just heard Paris's
     confession and given him the required shrift (absolution) –
     this service was usually offered in early morning. The two
     men are now conversing casually. The friar should, of course,
     make an important confession of his own to Paris ('I married
     the woman you intend to marry to another a few hours
     ago'). But he does not. He hopes Juliet will save him. He's a
     weak man, under his holy garb.*

107 *Paris does not ask what she is doing here (alone). He
     assumes she is just in the morning confession and shriving
     queue. He's not a very bright young man.*

108 *I.e. 'already a wife'.*

ACT 4, SCENE 1

Friar Lawrence's cell

FRIAR LAWRENCE
Thursday is quite short notice to be wed,
Art thou certain of Juliet's consent?[106]

PARIS
Her father hath agreed: that's enough for me.
I haven't had a chance to have a word
With my fair lady, for she doth naught but weep.
Weep, weep, thrice weep, and then she weeps
   some more
For Tybalt's death. In truth, I am annoyed.

FRIAR LAWRENCE (*aside*)
More tears there will be ere this week is run.
Here comes the lady, tell her how you feel.[107]

Enter Juliet

PARIS
My lady! Soon to be trouble and strife;
I bet you cannot wait till Thursday comes.

JULIET
That may be, sir, when I may be a wife.[108]

109 *She hasn't, of course, but she will not lie. She riddles, instead.*

110 *She loves – dutifully, not passionately – the listening friar, her 'father'. She cries; Paris misinterprets.*

111 *Sexual innuendo – covered by the decent prevarication that he will come early for the marriage preparations.*

112 *Holy, because they are in the celibate friar's cell. Sacred ground. It is made clear later on that the Paris–Juliet match will be a very large public event.*

PARIS

Come you to make confession to this father?

JULIET

To answer that, I should confess to you.[109]

PARIS

Do not deny to him that you love me.

JULIET

I will confess to you that I love him.[110]

PARIS

E'en though you weep, you bring me tears of joy.

JULIET

God give me strength, there's none so dim as him.

PARIS

Juliet, on Thursday early will I rouse[111] you:
Till then, adieu; and keep this holy kiss.[112]

Exit Paris

JULIET

Father, this kiss is kiss of death to me;
Come weep with me, past hope, past cure, past help!

113   The marriage has already been announced with banns in church. A Sunday has intervened in the four-day progress of the play. Why are the Capulets in such a hurry – has the nurse said something to them?

114   Interesting that she has brought a knife with her. There would hardly be one available in the friar's cell.

115   There's much use of sleeping draughts in this play, all supplied by Friar Feelgood Lawrence. His potion which produces corpse-like symptoms for many hours is pharmaceutical fiction. Iago mentions the standard sleeping medications of the period in Othello when he says, 'Not poppy, nor mandragora, / Nor all the drowsy syrups of the world, / Shall ever medicine thee to that sweet sleep / Which thou owedst yesterday.' The friar would have got opium from local poppies (which grow well in the heat of Italy). Mandragora, better known as mandrake, is a root common in Mediterranean countries that also has narcotic properties.

116   We are reminded that when we first encountered him, the friar, a good Franciscan in touch with the natural world, was gathering herbs. He has, given his knowledge of things botanical, a poison cabinet and a collection of medicinally useful drugs.

117   Those of a curious disposition may wonder why Romeo hasn't already done this or what his plan may be. By 'find Romeo' the friar means 'find out where he is hiding in Mantua'. With just two days to play with, and Mantua thirty miles away, this information will not be easily come by. An Elizabethan audience, of course, might have thought that the two city-states were only a couple of miles apart.

FRIAR LAWRENCE

I'm struggling now, I am at my wits' end.
From these banns there is no sure escape.[113]

JULIET

Holy Father, that's not what I would hear,
My dearest hope was you would have a plan
To set me free from this unholy mess.
If wife to Paris is all you can bring
I will unsheath this knife and slit my wrists.[114]

FRIAR LAWRENCE

Hold on a sec, I might just have a plan:
It's a long shot, yet one that might just work.
Take thou this vial and swallow it at night;
'Tis heavy gear, better than Seconal,[115]
That will knock you out for two full days.[116]
In that time thou wilt be pronounced dead
And placed into the vault of Capulet.
While you're crashed out, I will find Romeo
So he can drag you back to Mantua.[117]

JULIET

Thou art a good, dear father, thanks a lot;
With Lady Luck, I might escape this plot.

118 *We should imagine her kneeling before her father here. Faux submission. She is cunning, as well as more intelligent than any other Capulet.*

119 *But not 'I do love him well'. There is the odd suspicion lurking here that Juliet has not previously met Paris (as she had not, until the fateful evening when they fell in love, met Romeo). For a small town, the Veronese do rather keep themselves to themselves. And where, one can't help wondering, is Rosaline all this while? The invisible woman. Did Romeo invent her?*

ACT 4, SCENE 2

Capulet's mansion

CAPULET

So little time, so many preparations,
I wish I'd ordered in some caterers
And that my daughter was not in a grump.

Enter Juliet

CAPULET

What's that I see, a smile upon thy face?
Well that's a pleasant change and no mistake.

JULIET

My lesson hath been learned, I do repent.
To do thy bidding is my only will.[118]
I met dear Paris at the friar's cell
And there did think that I could love him well.[119]

CAPULET

That is good news. I knew you would relent.
Let's not till Thursday wait for your big day:
Tomorrow shall ye wed ere close of play.

120 The nurse is not on the scene. As already mentioned, Juliet can no longer entirely trust her.

121 The same thought will have flashed through the audience's mind – but the goodness of the friar has been stressed.

122 Grisly thought: bodies decompose fast in the heat of an Italian summer. Tybalt's corpse, in the Capulet vault, will by now be very ripe.

ACT 4, SCENE 3

Juliet's bedroom

LADY CAPULET
What, are you busy, could you use some help?

JULIET
No, Madam, I have packed and need some sleep.

LADY CAPULET
Then I will off to bed. Sleep, my dear.[120]

Exit Lady Capulet

JULIET
Farewell! God knows when we shall meet again.
A phantom fear doth chill and thrill my veins.
What if the holy friar played me false
And these capsules are not barbiturates
But something anodyne that will not work,
Or something deadly from which I'll not wake?[121]
Yet he's a holy man and must act true.
How if I wake among Tybalt's remains
And be afeared before Romeo comes?[122]
Choice have I none but my fate to accept.
Romeo, Romeo, Romeo! – I drink to thee.

Juliet falls upon the bed, unconscious

123 There is a lot of scene shifting in the original play between the mansions. It would, as noted earlier, be signalled to the audience by hanging flags. Between scenes the audience would see stage hands (perhaps in costume) coming on to put them up.

124 The first cock crow was at midnight. The second at three a.m. The third at dawn. Proverbial. No one ever got round to informing the cocks that they were alarm clocks with feathers. It's an allusion to Matthew, 26:34, in which Jesus predicts to Peter that he will betray him three times before the cock crows. Ominous.

125 An insinuation that there may have been a stag night, at which Capulet was present, with the ritual misbehaviour of men before the great event, on their last night of freedom.

ACT 4, SCENE 4

A room in Capulet's mansion [123]

CAPULET

    Come, stir, stir, stir! The second cock hath crow'd,
    There's much to do before the wedding feast,
    After which one more cock will surely crow. [124]

LADY CAPULET

    Thou hast a filthy mind. I'll have thee know
    Thy cock hath been in cases untoward. [125]

CAPULET

    Do not today bring up my faithlessness,
    This day is one of joy and happiness.
    Go waken Juliet, go and trim her up;
    I'll go and chat with Paris: hie, make haste.

126 Oddly, the nurse seems unaware of the fact that Juliet has already enjoyed a night of marital bliss. Where has the old biddy been all this time? It would be her responsibility to change the sheets – which might (after a legitimate first night of marriage) be hanged bloodstained outside the window, witness to the wife's pre-marital purity.

127 And the nurse will imminently join Verona's unemployed – which perhaps adds to her anguished shriek.

128 Is Juliet, one wonders, half-conscious? Listening to what is being said in a vegetative paralytic state?

129 It's not technically a lie – she's a corpse prepared for the funeral service. The friar is playing a very deep game, which could, when it all comes out, cost him his own life.

ACT 4, SCENE 5

Juliet's bedroom

NURSE
  Mistress, wake up! It is thy wedding day.
  'Tis good thou slept so long and deep last night;
  This night thou will have little time for that.[126]

Draws back the curtains

NURSE
  Alas, alas! Help, help! My lady's dead![127]

Enter Lady Capulet

LADY CAPULET
  Alack the day, she's dead, she's dead, she's dead!

Enter Capulet

CAPULET
  Away from her, I need to feel her pulse:
  I fear you're right, her body is quite cold.[128]
  My grief ties up my tongue, I cannot speak.

Enter Friar Lawrence, Paris and musicians

FRIAR LAWRENCE
  Come, is the bride ready to go to church?[129]

130   *Both Montague and Capulet families have only a single offspring: something which adds to the grief of their respective bereavements. But the lack of other male children – hungry for vengeance – holds out the possibility of eventual peace. Blood feuds require blood offspring to keep the conflict going.*

131   *This verbiage makes clear that Paris is a much shallower lover than Romeo.*

132   *The so-called Pauline consolation against grieving. Note that the friar does not enquire how Juliet died (no one does). No one examines the suspicious glass she drank the knockout drug from. Or wonders whether some criminal poisoned her – the nurse would be the obvious suspect. Crime scene investigation? Forget it.*

CAPULET

My tongue's untied, I find I can now speak.
She will to church, but not for her wedding.
Death is my son-in-law, death is my heir,
My daughter's dead, a funeral we prepare.[130]

LADY CAPULET

Accursed, unhappy, wretched, hateful day!
Our child from us hath been taken away.

NURSE

O woe! O woeful, woeful, woeful day!
Most lamentable day, most woeful day!

PARIS

Beguiled, divorced, wronged, spited, slain!
Widower I am, wedded I am not.[131]

CAPULET

Despised, distressed, hated, martyr'd, kill'd!
And with my child my joys are buried.

FRIAR LAWRENCE

Shame on you all! No more of this self-pity.
Though thy child's dead, she hath no need of tears,
For she's in heaven now. Rejoice! Rejoice![132]
This mortal coil about we all do walk
Is merely death deferred, not life well lived.
So with lighter hearts, let's carry her away.

133   *A joyous serenade was planned. There was a music gallery in Verona's cathedral, which would certainly have been where the Paris–Juliet match was planned to be solemnised. The musicians are often left out in both senses – (1) from the ceremony, which is cancelled, and (2) from the fact that their little scene is routinely dropped in modern production. In the original production they may have offered a musical interval.*

CAPULET
   I do suppose you're right, yet can but grieve,
   For death so sudden cannot natural be.
   All things that we ordained festival
   Turn from their office to black funeral.

FRIAR LAWRENCE
   That is the spirit, now her spirit's flown,
   Death takes all and all must follow her.

Exeunt all but the musicians

FIRST MUSICIAN
   I don't suppose they will want us to play 'Zadok
   the Priest' now.[133]

SECOND MUSICIAN
   Does that mean we're going to have to learn
   something else?

FIRST MUSICIAN
   That shouldn't make any difference to you as you'd
   never got round to learning the Handel anyway.

SECOND MUSICIAN
   At least I'm in tune.

THIRD MUSICIAN
   Belt up, the pair of you. Look on the bright side.
   We'll still get fed.

134 *The stars, mentioned in the first chorus, are taking over. Henceforth everything is 'fateful' – the playing out of foretold, irresistible destiny.*

135 *Balthasar (not that his name matters) is Romeo's 'man' – personal servant. He is 'booted' (you can't wear spurs on regular footwear) because he has ridden, as fast as his horse can carry him, from Verona.*

136 *I.e. the family vault. Balthasar, as his misconceived jest makes clear, is nervous about delivering the awful news. Messengers get killed.*

ACT 5, SCENE 1

A street in Mantua

Enter Romeo

ROMEO
I dreamed a dream that some might call a 'mare,
Yet I did find it joyful and most sweet.
I dreamed my lady found me stone-cold dead
And with her kisses roused me to my feet..[134]

Enter Balthasar, booted[135]

ROMEO
News from Verona! How now, Balthasar?
How doth my lady? How is her CPR?

BALTHASAR
She is not well, but neither is she ill:
Her body sleeps in Capel's monument.[136]

ROMEO
This cannot be, my Juliet must live.

BALTHASAR
You don't look well yourself, pray rest awhile.

ROMEO
Fetch me some horses, to her side I'll ride.

137   He's not thinking entirely clearly. How will he have his body
      put to rest in the Capulet tomb? The other question running
      through the audience's mind is why has the friar not sent
      some communication, as he earlier said he would? Is he
      playing an even deeper game than the lovers think?

138   The apothecary, we are to assume, is not as skilled a druggist
      as the friar. But he has a handy poison to sell – if, that is, he
      is willing to be a possible accomplice to murder.

ROMEO

Well, Juliet, I will lie with thee tonight.
No chance my kisses will give thee thy life.
And so my extant life will be extinct,
Two lovers joined for all eternity.[137]
Yet what means should I use to kill myself?
Perhaps some decent drugs will do the trick.
A dealer in a crack-den I do know:
To him I'll go and buy a gram of smack;
If that won't do the trick, then nothing will.

Enter apothecary

ROMEO

How now, good dealer, art you carrying?
I need some heavy gear to do me in.

APOTHECARY

Don't talk so loud, there's feds on every street;
If they do hear us, I'll go down for sure.
But as it happens, I have just the stuff.
'Twill put you out for days, if not for years.[138]

Exit apothecary

ROMEO

Sounds just the job, my thanks to you, good man.
To trade in death is sometimes not all bad.
I will to Juliet's grave, there to repose.
Do your best, good drugs, make me comatose.

139 *We know little about Friar John except, we may deduce, that he may not be of the same (Franciscan) mendicant order as Lawrence. If he is already here from Mantua, he must have ridden – fast. Mendicant Franciscans went barefoot. They were not, by the rules of their order, riders of horses.*

140 *This seems untrue. We're free to come to our own conclusions. Principally that Friar John – on the priestly bush telegraph – couldn't be bothered to do what he was asked to. Or prudently did not want to get involved in an explosively dangerous situation.*

141 *If she'd been buried as a commoner – in a common coffin under six feet of earth – she would be dead by now. But she is lying in the family vault. It's hard to believe that, even in a vault, her body would be left, like a butcher's side of beef, on a slab, and not sealed in a lead coffin. There is some confusion here as to whether Juliet's body lies underground, or (as it is eventually revealed) above ground in the Capulet 'monument'.*

ACT 5, SCENE 2

Friar Lawrence's cell

Enter Friar John [139]

FRIAR JOHN
Good morrow, I from Mantua have come.

Enter Friar Lawrence

FRIAR LAWRENCE
Welcome, good brother, how was Romeo?
Has he writ a reply to my letter?

FRIAR JOHN
Once more the best laid plans of mice and men
Have gone astray. I fear the consequence.
A plague within the city did befall;
All doors were locked so I could not get in,
Thus Romeo never your letter got. [140]

Exit Friar John

FRIAR LAWRENCE
That is unfortunate and no mistake.
Within three hours will Juliet awake.
Finding herself alone inside the tomb,
To panic attacks she must sure succumb. [141]

142 *A mattock is a chisel, a wrenching iron a crowbar. One of
the tests of death was to hold a mirror in front of the mouth
and nose, to see if it misted with breathing. It's made clear
that Juliet's heart and lung functions have been wholly
suspended. Thanks to the friar's wonder drug, she has been
holding her breath for twelve hours.*

143 *Romeo's man is as characterless as the Capulets' Peter. Their
view of what is going on would be useful. Balthasar may be
a temporary hire. Digging up corpses could get him in big
trouble. He displays understandable nervousness on the edge
of things.*

144 *'Maw' = stomach. It's getting very physical – and, in a
flight of Romeo fancy, a kind of reverse birth process is
being played out. The maw is 'detestable' because it is
decomposing Juliet's body. One of the functions of vaults
(and lead-lined coffins) was to keep worms at bay. Made
things easier on Resurrection Day.*

ACT 5, SCENE 3

A churchyard, outside the tomb of the Capulets

Enter Paris

PARIS

    I come to whisper my fondest farewells
    Unto my bride who never was my bride.
    Beside her tomb, some flowers I shall lay;
    First to the shadows I retire to pray.

Retires
Enter Romeo and Balthasar

ROMEO

    Give me that mattock and the wrenching iron;[142]
    Into the tomb I'll break, not to exhume
    But lie beside the corpse of Juliet.
    I beg you take this letter to my dad
    And leave me here alone to my intent.

BALTHASAR

    Thy tone doth give me cause for much concern;
    I will pretend to go, but not too far.[143]

Balthasar retires

ROMEO

    Thou detestable maw, thou womb of death,
    Into thy jaws I shall impose myself.[144]

145 *Both men are armed with their trusty noblemen's rapiers. Paris, related as he is to the prince, intends a citizen's arrest, letting the city axeman do the dirty work. (Nobles were not hanged.)*

146 *The point is made that Paris is younger than Romeo – a mere boy.*

147 *Romeo's plan. There will be three of them in this union.*

Romeo begins to open the tomb

PARIS

Why, is that not the banished Montague?
'Tis not enough that he hath Tybalt slain
And caused my bride such grief that she too died.
He comes here to their tomb to mock and gloat.

Steps forth

PARIS

Condemnèd villain, I do apprehend thee:
Obey, and go with me; for thou must die.[145]

ROMEO

I must indeed; yet not at thy young hands,[146]
So kindly, if you please, leave me alone.
I have not come to pick a fight with thee,
So nip off home and have a cup of tea.

PARIS

I will not leave, I do prefer to fight.

ROMEO

So be it then, prepare for blackest night.

They fight

PARIS

I am slain. One last favour, if you please,
Open the tomb, lay me with Juliet.[147]

148 *It's dark(ish) and, too late, Romeo remembers who Paris is.
Balthasar, on their furious gallop back from Mantua, will
have told him about the Capulet marriage plans.*

149 *Preparation of bodies for eternal rest seems oddly
perfunctory in Verona.*

Paris dies

ROMEO

'Tis best to check and find out who I've killed.
Oh whoops, again too hasty have I been,
'Tis Paris, kinsman to Mercutio,[148]
Who was, I heard, to Juliet betrothed.
'Tis far too late to bring him back to life,
Though lying next to her is recompense.

Places Paris in the tomb

ROMEO

How oft when men are at the point of death
Have they been merry! Yet I cannot smile.
I gaze upon thy beauty, Juliet,
That even death itself dare not conquer.
For though thou lieth still and breatheth not,
There's crimson in thy lips and in thy cheeks.
If only I a paramedic were
I might then draw the right conclusion.
There is Tybalt wrapped in bloody sheets.[149]
I'm sorry that I killed thee; pardon me!
Death tries to take my wife to be his love.
Yet will I prevent this dateless bargain
For with my death, next Juliet I'll lie.
Here's to my love. O dealer, good and true,
Thy drugs are quick. Thus with a kiss I die.

Romeo dies

150 *He is tooled up to rescue Juliet – although how he intends to use a spade, shoeless, is not clear. Things are moving so fast the audience will not worry about such trifles.*

151 *The cowardly friar thinks, if Juliet is miraculously revived and her two lovers inexplicably dead, the whole thing may yet blow over and he can go back to gathering daisies and buttercups.*

Enter Friar Lawrence, with lantern, crowbar and spade[150]

FRIAR LAWRENCE
What light doth burn within the open tomb?

BALTHASAR
'Tis Romeo, he's been there half an hour.

FRIAR LAWRENCE
This place doth fill me with black foreboding,
I dare not bear to think what I may find.
Alas, there lies Romeo! Paris too!
This is much worse than in my darkest dreams.

Juliet wakes

JULIET
I do remember well where I should be,
And there I am. Where is my Romeo?

FRIAR LAWRENCE
Don't rise too quick; 'tis best you stay sat down,
My plan has not worked out as I had hoped.
Thy husband in thy bosom there lies dead
And Paris, too, he looketh not so good.
But you, at least, now breathe and have a pulse;
It's best to cut our losses, hie we hence.[151]

152 She wasn't buried with a dagger – it's Romeo's weapon, still dripping, perhaps, with Paris's blood.

153 The 'Roman death' – Juliet, to the end, impresses us with her courage. As predicted earlier (note 57), she kills herself, like Dido, with her lover's dagger (or her lover's sword, in Dido's case). Phallic.

154 Verona's not very impressive police force makes a belated entrance.

JULIET

I will not leave this place where Romeo
Hath overdosed. This tomb shall be our tomb.
I'm only sad he's taken all the drugs
So I must take this dagger to my breast.[152]

Takes Romeo's dagger

JULIET

This is thy sheath; there rust, and let me die.

Falls on Romeo's body and dies [153]
Enter Captain of the Watch [154]

CAPTAIN OF THE WATCH

This seems to be a multiple crime scene,
I'd best alert the prince and Capulets.

Enter prince

PRINCE

What's going on that drags me from my bed?

Enter Lord and Lady Capulet

CAPULET

We hear strange rumours about Juliet.

LADY CAPULET

Paris and Romeo are mentioned, too.

155 *She loves her son sufficiently to have died of grief. He never mentions or apparently thinks of her. In some textual versions of the play, Benvolio (never much of a presence) dies as well – cause unexplained.*

CAPTAIN OF THE WATCH
    A lie I cannot tell, they are all dead.

Lord and Lady Capulet enter the tomb

CAPULET
    What the captain says, it is all true,
    'Tis clear the blame lies with the Montagues.

Enter Montague

MONTAGUE
    Alas, my liege, my wife is dead tonight;
    Grief of my son's exile hath stopp'd her breath.[155]

Montague goes into the tomb

PRINCE
    Prepare yourself, my lord, things are much worse.

MONTAGUE
    I see that Romeo is also dead,
    The fault lies solely with the Capulets.

PRINCE
    Hold on! Hold on! I will investigate,
    These untimely deaths will not go unsolved.
    Doth anyone have crucial evidence?

156 The friar, cowardly or diplomatic, however you like to see
     him, ostentatiously avoids reference to the real cause of the
     lovers' deaths – the pointless feud between the Montagues
     and Capulets, which is tearing the city apart.

157 The prince is not a man to take time over his judgments or
     to worry that one of his kinsmen has been brutally murdered
     – on sacred ground, no less. It's worth noting that the friar
     does not himself expect to live much longer. It's hard to
     think, whatever his future, that it will lie in Verona. He's up
     to his armpits in misdeeds.

FRIAR LAWRENCE

    Good prince, I can explain it all,
    The fault it lies with no one, yet with all.
    These deaths were naught but sad coincidence.[156]
    Please bear with me, as I do tell my tale,
    For it is long and stretches all belief.
    To start at the beginning, I did wed
    My lord Romeo and sweet Juliet.
    Their wedding was a secret kept from all
    Because the families were enemies.
    That was tricky, but then things got worse
    When Tybalt picked a fight and wound up killed
    While Romeo to Mantua was sent.

PRINCE

    You're going on a bit, pray make this brief.

FRIAR LAWRENCE

    I'll do my best to cut this story short.
    Suffice to say, some letters went astray,
    So everybody died. And that's that.

PRINCE

    Thou art a holy man who speaks the truth.
    I rule that there is blame on either side.
    The lesson to be learned is simply this:
    That hatchets are best buried in the ground,
    And not in one another's back or neck.[157]

158 *Almost certainly Shakespeare wants us to see this as a wholly inadequate reparation – the older generation has learned nothing.*

159 *It's not just the lovers – the flower of Verona's youth has been rubbed out by clan feud and gang warfare: Tybalt, Mercutio, Benvolio (?), Romeo, Paris. The prince's word 'glooming' is appropriate, and gloom is the mood of the end of the play. It's a powerful theatrical effect. One imagines the audience leaving in sombre silence.*

CAPULET

O brother Montague, give me thy hand.

MONTAGUE

And let us build a statue in pure gold
To honour Romeo and Juliet.[158]

PRINCE

A glooming peace this morning with it brings;
Let's hope it stays that way for all our sakes:
For never was a story of more woe
Than this of Juliet and her Romeo.[159]

John Crace is the *Guardian*'s parliamentary sketch writer and author of the 'Digested Read' column, and he writes regularly for *Grazia*. He is the author of *I Never Promised You a Rose Garden: A Short Guide to Modern Politics, the Coalition and the General Election* and also *Baby Alarm: A Neurotic's Guide to Fatherhood*; *Vertigo: One Football Fan's Fear of Success*; *Harry's Games: Inside the Mind of Harry Redknapp*; *Brideshead Abbreviated: The Digested Read of the Twentieth Century* and *The Digested Twenty-first Century*.

John Sutherland is Lord Northcliffe Professor Emeritus of Modern English Literature at University College London and previously taught at the California Institute of Technology. He writes regularly for the *Guardian* and *The Times* and is the author of many books, including *Curiosities of Literature*, *Henry V, War Criminal?* (with Cedric Watts), biographies of Walter Scott, Stephen Spender and the Victorian elephant Jumbo, and *The Boy Who Loved Books*, a memoir.

TRANSWORLD PUBLISHERS
61–63 Uxbridge Road, London W5 5SA
www.transworldbooks.co.uk

Transworld is part of the Penguin Random House group of companies
whose addresses can be found at global.penguinrandomhouse.com

Penguin
Random House
UK

First published in Great Britain in 2016 by Doubleday
an imprint of Transworld Publishers

A CIP catalogue record for this book
is available from the British Library.

ISBN 9780857524256

Typeset in 11/13pt Berylium by Julia Lloyd Design
Printed and bound by Clays Ltd, Bungay, Suffolk.

Penguin Random House is committed to a sustainable
future for our business, our readers and our planet. This book
is made from Forest Stewardship Council® certified paper.

MIX
Paper from
responsible sources
FSC® C018179

1 3 5 7 9 10 8 6 4 2